S0-AYQ-167

CHILDREN'S ILLUSTRATORS

MARLA FRAZEE

Sheila Griffin Llanas
ABDO Publishing Company

visit us at
www.abdopublishing.com

Published by ABDO Publishing Company, PO Box 398166, Minneapolis, MN 55439. Copyright © 2012 by Abdo Consulting Group, Inc. International copyrights reserved in all countries. No part of this book may be reproduced in any form without written permission from the publisher. The Checkerboard Library™ is a trademark and logo of ABDO Publishing Company.

Printed in the United States of America, North Mankato, Minnesota.
102011
012012

 PRINTED ON RECYCLED PAPER

Cover Photo: courtesy Marla Frazee
Interior Photos: courtesy Marla Frazee pp. 5, 6, 7, 10, 11, 13, 16, 17; Getty Images p. 18
    Book cover from *Roller Coaster*, copyright © 2003 by Marla Frazee, reproduced by permission of Houghton Mifflin Harcourt Publishing Company. This material may not be reproduced in any form or by any means without the prior written permission of the publisher. p. 9
    Book cover from *That Kookoory!*, copyright © 1995 by Margaret Walden Froehlich, reproduced by permission of Houghton Mifflin Harcourt Publishing Company. This material may not be reproduced in any form or by any means without the prior written permission of the publisher. p. 15
    Illustration from *A Couple of Boys Have the Best Week Ever*, copyright © 2008 by Marla Frazee, reprinted by permission of Houghton Mifflin Harcourt Publishing Company. This material may not be reproduced in any form or by any means without the prior written permission of the publisher. p. 19
    Reprinted with the permission of Beach Lane Books, an imprint of Simon & Schuster Children's Publishing Division from *All the World* by Liz Garton Scanlon, illustrated by Marla Frazee. Illustrations copyright © 2009 Marla Frazee. pp. 20–21

Series Coordinator: BreAnn Rumsch / Editors: Megan M. Gunderson, BreAnn Rumsch
Art Direction: Neil Klinepier

Library of Congress Cataloging-in-Publication Data

Llanas, Sheila Griffin, 1958-
 Marla Frazee / Sheila Griffin Llanas.
    p. cm. -- (Children's illustrators)
 Includes index.
 ISBN 978-1-61783-246-8
 1. Frazee, Marla--Juvenile literature. 2. Illustrators--United States--Biography--Juvenile literature. I. Frazee, Marla. II. Title.
 NC975.5.F69L59 2012
 741.6'42--dc23
 [B]
                            2011027842

CONTENTS

STORIES IN THE ART

Marla Frazee always knew what she wanted to be when she grew up. When she was two years old, she drew a picture of a cat. At least, it looked like a cat to her! Some people said it looked like a spider, while others thought it was a ghost.

Frazee still has the drawing because it means a lot to her. It reminds her that she has been an artist her whole life. That cat picture was the start of her career. Frazee published her first book in 1990. Since then, she has brought more than 15 picture books to life with her vibrant art. Two of them have even been named **Caldecott Honor Books**.

One reason Frazee's books are popular is that she understands her audience. She knows that older children read words. But younger children "read" pictures. Frazee's illustrations tell detailed stories that children love to explore.

At home in California, Frazee is close to what she loves most. There, she enjoys family and friends, the ocean, the mountains, and her community. Frazee likes to walk on the beach and hike in the hills. In her **diverse** neighborhood, she shops at **ethnic** food markets and antique stores. However, Frazee's favorite place to be is at home in her art studio creating new books.

Frazee draws inspiration from her surroundings. Fans hope she'll be inspired for years to come!

FAMILY CONNECTION

Marla Frazee was born on January 16, 1958, in Los Angeles, California. Marla's father, Gerald, was a businessman. Her mother, Nancy, was a teacher. Marla grew up with an older brother and a younger sister.

Marla's childhood unfolded in the center of a large extended family. They always lived in or around Los Angeles.

Frazee has always lived in California near her childhood home. She does not want to live anywhere else!

Her grandparents and other family members had immigrated to the United States from Lebanon. They settled in California in the 1920s.

Marla's relatives liked to gather around large meals. Her grandmother often cooked Arabic meals for the whole family. She made foods such as stuffed grape leaves and stuffed zucchini.

When she was at her grandmother's house, Marla liked to help in the kitchen. Every night, her grandmother wiped the stove, covered it, and turned on the light above the burners. It was as if she were tucking the stove into bed. Marla told her grandmother how much she loved the stove. Her grandmother said, "Then it will be yours one day." Today, the beautiful stove is nestled in Marla's own kitchen.

An Artist Emerges

Growing up, Marla was quiet and shy. Activities such as attending sleepovers and riding roller coasters made her nervous. Instead, Marla loved to climb trees, ride her bike, and do puzzles. But mostly, Marla read books and drew pictures.

At Rhoda Street Elementary School in Encino, California, Marla especially loved making art. One day, she was working on painting a portrait. At one point, she noticed she had accidentally used blue paint on the face!

Marla was surprised to hear her teachers praise her for making a shadow under the chin. This lesson helped Marla grow as an artist. She learned that it's okay to make mistakes.

Marla also spent hours studying two of her favorite books. One was *Where the Wild Things Are* by Maurice Sendak. Sendak's book is about a boy named Max. In the story, Max's bedroom becomes a forest! Marla thought this was amazing.

In some books, Frazee explores fears and anxieties she had as a child.

The other book was Robert McCloskey's *Blueberries for Sal.* McCloskey's main character, Sal, has messy hair and wears overalls and sandals. These details **enchanted** Marla.

Marla studied the styles of both artists. She appreciated the magical way Sendak's scenes changed. And she noticed that McCloskey's images featured only blueberry-colored ink. Marla wanted to someday design a book's scenes and choose its colors. She was only in second grade. But she already knew that one day she would illustrate children's books, too.

CREATIVE DREAMS

When Marla was in third grade, her best friend Lisa wrote a story. Lisa asked Marla to illustrate it. The two friends attached the finished pages together with brass brads to make a book. They called it *The Friendship Circle*.

Lisa and Marla's teachers entered *The Friendship Circle* in the California State Fair, where it won an award. The

The Friendship Circle

Written by Lisa Gilden

Illustrated by Marla Frazee

girls were proud of their book. The librarian even requested a copy for the school. So, Lisa and Marla got to work for the second time. When it was finished, the librarian put the book on a library shelf.

In 1976, Marla graduated from Glendale High School. She was ready to pursue her dreams! So she began attending Art Center College of Design, in Pasadena, California. Marla studied illustration at Art Center. She enjoyed her classes there.

Marla earned her bachelo of fine arts degree in 1981. days after graduating, she beg a job at Walt Disney Studios. She worked in animation and made **storyboard** sketches. It was a good job, but Marla quit after only six weeks. She really wanted to create her own art.

...sa

BREAKTHROUGH!

Frazee loved life in Pasadena. She decided to settle down there with her husband, Tim Bradley. The two had met at Art Center and then married in 1982. Eventually, they had three sons named Graham, Reed, and James.

Meanwhile, Frazee found work as a **freelance artist**. She drew illustrations for toy companies such as Mattel. She also designed boxes for McDonald's Happy Meals and Kellogg's cereals. These projects were easy to get and they paid well. Frazee also loved working from home.

But, Frazee still dreamed of illustrating children's books. Yet when she showed her **portfolio** to publishers, they turned her down. Editors said her artwork was too commercial, too slick. It was not personal enough. Frazee wondered what it would take to make art for children's books.

Finally, an editor at Harper and Row named Linda Zuckerman liked Frazee's work. Zuckerman asked her to illustrate a picture book by Sue Alexander. In 1990, *World Famous Muriel and the Magic Mystery* was published. Frazee's career was on its way! At least, it seemed to be.

Frazee calls her studio her oasis. It is her favorite place to be.

PICTURE BOOKS GALORE

Five years went by without another book illustration job. Frazee wondered what she was doing wrong. She began to think carefully about her art style. She knew how to make illustrations for advertisements and toy companies. Finally, she realized that illustrations in children's books were different.

In picture books, words tell one story and illustrations tell another. The two stories come together on the pages of the book. Frazee understood that she needed her drawings to tell stories.

Frazee's next opportunity to illustrate a picture book came in 1995. *That Kookoory!* by Margaret Walden Froehlich is the story of a rooster that crows about a town fair. He is so excited that he doesn't notice a weasel following him. This time, Frazee's colorful paintings told many stories. Her illustrations earned rave reviews.

THAT KOOKOORY!

WRITTEN BY *Margaret Walden Froehlich*

ILLUSTRATED BY
Marla Frazee

The third book Frazee illustrated was a lot of work! *The Seven Silly Eaters* by Mary Ann Hoberman has nine characters, a bunch of pets, and a busy house. Frazee brought them all to life with her detailed imagination. Additional projects soon included *Harriet, You'll Drive Me Wild!* by Mem Fox and *Mrs. Biddlebox* by Linda Smith. Frazee's childhood dream had finally become a reality.

IN THE STUDIO

With her career on track, Frazee soon got into a routine. In the mornings, she takes her dog Rocket for a walk in the mountains near her house. Back home, she heads to her art studio. It is a tiny cabin in the backyard, shaded by an avocado tree. There, she draws and paints all day.

To start a new book, Frazee makes **thumbnail** sketches and decides how one picture will follow another. Next, she makes a **dummy** to help her figure out how her pictures will work with the words.

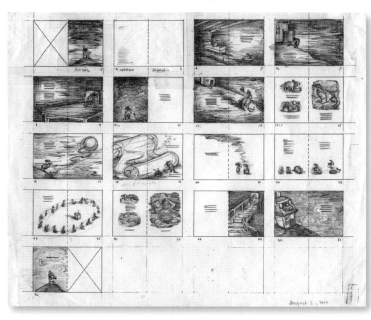

*Frazee's thumbnails for **Mrs. Biddlebox** show scenes with dark swirls. These strengthen the story's mood.*

Then, Frazee considers the characters. What do they look like? Where do they live? How do they act? When she answers those questions, her characters seem to come to life. Frazee recalls how much she loved McCloskey's *Blueberries for Sal*. She wants her characters to be just as lovable as Sal.

Frazee develops a **unique** style for every book. Still, she usually works with black pencil and transparent inks. Her paper, brushes, and paints are important. However, she believes her best tools are her ideas. These can come in a flash! But sometimes, it takes years for them to become books.

A character sketch created for
The Boss Baby, *published in 2010*

ELEMENTS OF ART: COMPOSITION

Composition is one of the basic parts of art. It is the arrangement of forms, lines, and colors within the frame of a picture. Composition plays a big role in how a finished picture feels.

Frazee spends a good deal of time working out where to place each element of her drawings. She adds a lot of details for readers to discover. In many of Frazee's books, such as *The Seven Silly Eaters* and *All the World*, these details add depth to the story.

FAMILY FUN

Frazee gets many book ideas from her own family and home life. During one family vacation, her sons were obsessed with roller coasters. That gave Frazee the idea for her book *Roller Coaster*. It was the first book she both wrote and illustrated.

To research the book, Frazee had to face her fears about roller coasters. So, she tested some out with her sons. During the rides, she threw her arms into the air to see how it felt. The book has few words. However, the people's faces tell the story as they ride the zipping and looping roller coaster!

Frazee's next book, *Santa Claus: The World's Number One Toy Expert*, was published in 2005. Then

Between 2006 and 2010, Frazee illustrated four Clementine books.

in 2006, the adorable *Clementine* premiered. Frazee illustrated this character for a novel series by Sara Pennypacker.

Frazee's career was doing well. But one day, she was feeling overwhelmed. So she thought, just take baby steps. This pep talk gave Frazee an idea for a book. The result was *Walk On!*, published in 2006.

In **A Couple of Boys,** *readers discover that "nature camp" is actually a week at the beach with Eamon's grandparents.*

Around that same time, Frazee's family inspired her once again. Her son James spent a week at nature camp with his friend Eamon. When he came home, they all drew pictures of the week and made it into a silly book. Eventually, Frazee turned those pictures into *A Couple of Boys Have the Best Week Ever*. In 2009, the book won a **Caldecott Honor**.

WONDERFUL WORLD

In 2007, Frazee's editor had sent her an inspiring manuscript called "All the World" by Liz Garton Scanlon. Frazee loved the brief text that celebrated family, nature, and community.

Frazee was excited to illustrate it. She tried many sketches until she struck the right combination. Her illustrations follow several families that live along California's central coast, a place Frazee loves. The art is full of humor, warmth, and love.

It usually takes Frazee a full year to illustrate a picture book. It feels rewarding to finish a book and exciting

All the world
is old and new

to start the next one. *All the World* was published in 2009. Readers everywhere adored it! In 2010, it earned Frazee her second **Caldecott Honor**. That same year, Frazee published the funny picture book, *Boss Baby*. And, she began working on illustrations for *Stars* by Mary Lyn Ray.

In addition to her art, Frazee also teaches classes at the Art Center. She calls her classroom a "picture book illustration laboratory." There, she teaches her students all she has learned.

Today, Frazee still lives near her childhood home. She puts her heart into her home and her family. When she is in her studio, she puts all she loves into her art. It's no wonder that readers everywhere connect to the warmth in Frazee's work.

Readers young and old love Frazee's peaceful, expansive paintings in **All the World.**

GLOSSARY

Caldecott Honor Book - a runner-up to the Caldecott Medal. The Caldecott Medal is an award the American Library Association gives to the artist who illustrated the year's best picture book.

diverse - made up of unlike pieces or qualities.

dummy - a manuscript laid out in book form, with sketches and finished samples of all the illustrations.

enchant - to attract and hold someone's attention by being interesting or pretty.

ethnic - of or relating to groups of people organized by race, nationality, religion, or culture.

freelance artist - an artist without a long-term commitment to a single employer.

portfolio - a selection of work, especially of drawings, paintings, or photographs. It may be presented to show one's skill as an artist.

storyboard - a series of drawings or pictures that show the changes of scenes and actions for a movie, television show, or commercial.

thumbnail - a small, rough sketch drawn by an artist before he or she makes the full-sized sketch.

unique - being the only one of its kind.

WEB SITES

To learn more about Marla Frazee, visit ABDO Publishing Company online. Web sites about Marla Frazee are featured on our Book Links page. These links are routinely monitored and updated to provide the most current information available.
www.abdopublishing.com

INDEX